The Incredible yet True Adventures of Alexander von Humboldt

The INCREDIBLE yet TRUE
Adventures of

ALEXANDER
VON HUMBOLDT

*The Greatest Inventor-Naturalist-
Scientist-Explorer Who Ever Lived*

VOLKER MEHNERT

Illustrated by **CLAUDIA LIEB**

Translated by Becky L. Crook

THE EXPERIMENT

NEW YORK

Thanks to Dr. Tobias Kraft, manager for the production of the German edition of this book, and the Berlin-Brandenburg Academy of Science for fact-checking the information herein.

The Experiment, LLC
220 East 23rd Street, Suite 600
New York, NY 10010-4658
theexperimentpublishing.com

THE EXPERIMENT and its colophon are registered trademarks of The Experiment, LLC. Many of the designations used by manufacturers and sellers to distinguish their products are claimed as trademarks. Where those designations appear in this book and The Experiment was aware of a trademark claim, the designations have been capitalized.

The Experiment's books are available at special discounts when purchased in bulk for premiums and sales promotions as well as for fund-raising or educational use. For details, contact us at info@theexperimentpublishing.com.

The translation of this work was supported by a grant from the Goethe-Institut.

GOETHE INSTITUT

Library of Congress Cataloging-in-Publication Data available upon request

ISBN 978-1-61519-631-9
Ebook ISBN 978-1-61519-632-6

Cover and text design by Beth Bugler
Illustrations by Claudia Lieb
Translated by Becky L. Crook

Manufactured in China

First printing September 2019
10 9 8 7 6 5 4 3 2 1

Contents

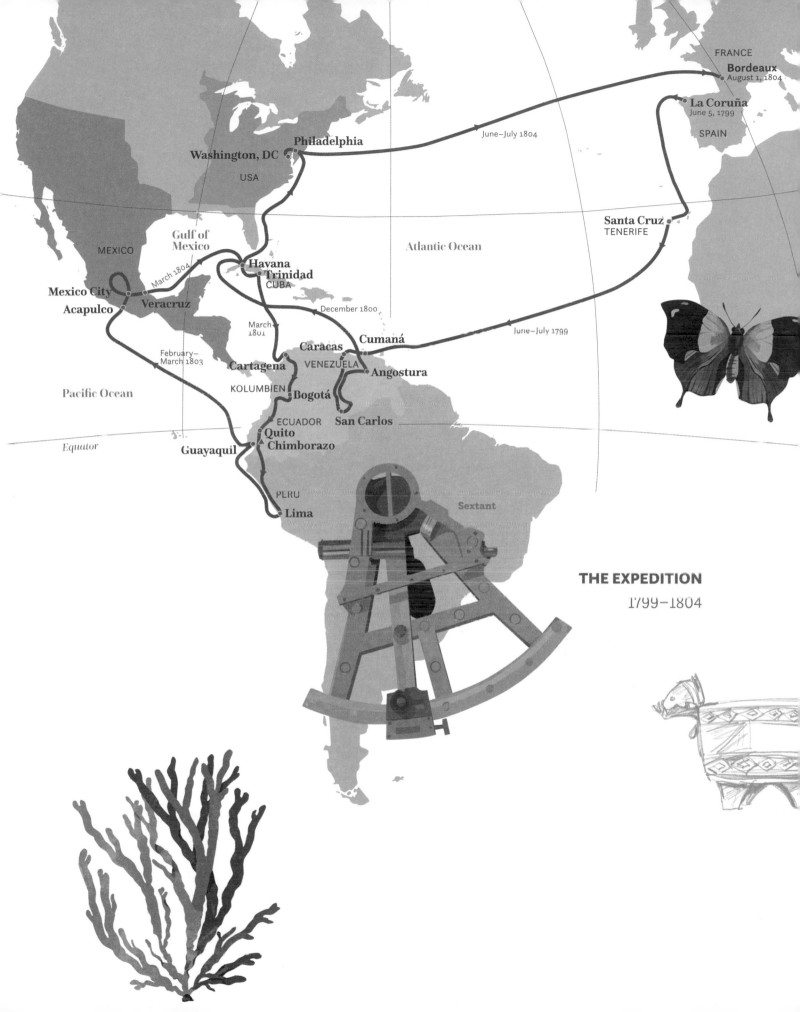

FRANCE

Bordeaux
August 1, 1804

La Coruña
June 5, 1799

SPAIN

Philadelphia

Washington, DC

USA

June–July 1804

Santa Cruz
TENERIFE

Atlantic Ocean

Gulf of
Mexico

March 1804

Havana
Trinidad
CUBA

MEXICO

Mexico City

Acapulco

Veracruz

December 1800

Cumaná

June–July 1799

March
1801

Caracas

VENEZUELA

Angostura

Pacific Ocean

February–
March 1803

Cartagena

KOLUMBIEN

Bogotá

San Carlos

ECUADOR

Quito

Guayaquil

Chimborazo

Equator

PERU

Lima

Sextant

THE EXPEDITION

1799–1804

PROLOGUE

December 1827, in the Prussian capital of Berlin. Crowds have gathered in front of the university. There is so much chaos in the neighboring streets that even police on horseback cannot break up the throng. Normally there would only be a few professors and their students—but today there are hundreds, perhaps even thousands of people pushing to get in. What is going on?

A man is giving a lecture and half the city is eager to hear him. Nothing like this has ever happened before. The man's name is Alexander von Humboldt and his speech is neither boring nor bookish. On the contrary, he is a mesmer-izing storyteller. He speaks freely to the crowd without using notes. Humboldt is talking about his adventures across North and South America, through tropical jungles, to the tops of volcanoes, and crossing paths with new and interesting people he's never seen before. But he also has exciting new knowledge to share about the oceans and cosmos, geology and climate, magnetism and electricity.

Humboldt has been lecturing several times a week for half a year and word of his captivating presentations has spread throughout the city. Everyone wants to catch a glimpse of the famous explorer, to hear him speak, and everyone wants to get a good seat. The people come from every walk of life: teachers and students, craftspeople and laborers. Even the king of Prussia attends. Women, who were not allowed to attend universities in those days, are also permitted to come. The lectures are free. And the lucky attendees leave awestruck every time. It's no wonder that the university lecture halls are soon bursting at the seams and Humboldt has to relocate to a nearby public concert hall with room for a thousand listeners.

A groundbreaking transformation is underway: The study of science, previously conducted behind closed doors and discussed only by a select few, has suddenly become more accessible and understandable for anyone. And the blazing hero of this revolution is none other than Alexander von Humboldt, who will come to be known as one of the most famous scientists of the century—in spite of the fact that, as a young boy, he was somewhat less promising. . . .

Chapter 1

An Adventurous Boy

"Have you been poking around in the garden again with the beetles and flowers?" the strict tutor asked the young boy. Alexander was supposed to have his nose buried in books, but the young man thought that rocks, insects, and plants were so much more interesting. His grades were mediocre at best, to the point that his parents even worried he might not be very smart. They often compared him with his brother, Wilhelm, which wasn't fair at all. His tutor made him do the exact same lessons as his studious brother, even though Wilhelm was two years older. It was simply impossible for Alexander to keep up. Yet even though he was shy and sometimes sickly, he was actually a good learner.

At heart, however, he was interested in other things. While Wilhelm was happy to study languages like Latin and Greek and to read about literature and philosophy, Alexander was more curious about plants, animals, and nature in general. The quiet, slender boy went out in search of creatures in the large park that surrounded the Humboldt family's small castle in Berlin. Alexander's father was an officer and chamberlain at the court of the Prussian king and so could afford such a splendid residence and property, which Alexander couldn't help but explore.

As he got older, Alexander continued to spend as much time outside as possible. He was always on the move. "That boy loves adventuring," his tutor complained. Alexander's curiosity drew him again and again to the city botanical gardens, where he marveled at the palms and other gigantic trees from tropical regions while dreaming of faraway lands. Oh, how he wished he could see these plants in their native soil!

At home, he pored over every book by brave travelers and groundbreaking explorers that he could get his hands on. He especially liked the adventures of the British explorer James Cook. But sadly, after the sudden death of his father, his strict mother took over his education. Alexander had to put aside his daydreams of botany and world travel and focus instead on his studies: state finance and economics.

It wasn't until Alexander was a student at the University of Göttingen that he would finally be able to pursue his passion. There, Alexander was delighted to meet a man who had sailed with Cook for three years: Georg Forster. No other German had seen as much of the world. Forster's book of travel narratives was a hit. His tales of experiences in far-off lands and unknown islands in the South Sea fanned the flames of Alexander's wanderlust.

Alexander began by first visiting places close to home. Together with Georg, he journeyed to France, the Netherlands, and England. In London, England's capital, he was especially intrigued by all the ships that were docked in the bay. Their cargo included sugar, tea, spices, and other wares from the farthest reaches of the earth. Alexander's longing for travel grew bigger and bigger.

THE FAMOUS BROTHER

Wilhelm von Humboldt did not travel around the world like his brother, Alexander, but he was an esteemed scholar. At the age of thirteen, he was already fluent in Latin, Greek, and French and he went on to learn English, Italian, Spanish, Czech, and Hungarian. As a diplomat in the Prussian civil service, he negotiated with foreign governments in Paris, Rome, and Vienna. Back in Berlin, he served as minister of education for a modernized school system. He also founded the first city university, which was renamed after him and his brother in 1949: Humboldt University of Berlin.

"From the earliest age, I had a burning desire to travel to distant lands and places rarely visited by other Europeans."

When he came back to Germany, Alexander once again had to put his dreams on hold. His mother wouldn't tolerate any further escapades. "You need to get a dependable job," she demanded. She expected Alexander to have a career as an officer in the Prussian civil service, like his father. Not wanting to disappoint, Alexander decided to continue his education at the Mining Academy in Freiburg. At least here he would be able to study the natural sciences.

He was fascinated by everything that took place in the belly of the earth. It wasn't enough for him to learn about such things from books and teachers. Alexander had to go to the mines, where he could creep and crawl through their dark narrow shafts. He was transfixed, drawn to the subterranean rocks, metals, minerals, and gases. He examined every detail of the materials.

By the time he was only twenty-two years old, Alexander had finished his studies and gotten a job as a mining inspector. His task was to monitor coal, salt, and gold mines and to increase their yields. He was a restless young man, so while doing his job he also wrote textbooks and even started a new school for miners.

PRUSSIA

At the end of the eighteenth century, Germany was divided between multiple small states and principalities. Through military strength and skillful diplomacy, the Prussian kingdom was able to gain more power over time. Small states in the north and east were either conquered or entered the union voluntarily. After Bayern, Baden, and Württemberg joined, the German Reich was formed in 1871 and the Prussian king Wilhelm was crowned emperor of Germany.

He began to discover that he was good at inventing things: Alexander developed a new type of mining lamp and a breathing mask—tools that helped miners in their dangerous work. He was quickly promoted and his future as a civil servant seemed bright. As a Prussian official, he now wore a uniform.

The daydreaming young Alexander had become the esteemed Baron von Humboldt. He might even one day be a minister in the king's court!

But then, in 1796, his mother died after a long battle with cancer. Both brothers inherited a large fortune. Of course, all of his relatives were furious when Alexander promptly quit his job. "I'm off," he announced, "to travel the world and sail across oceans."

Doing so, however, was going to prove more challenging than he could imagine.

Chapter 2

FAREWELL, EUROPE
Which way to the Americas?

Straw electrometer to detect electric charges

Alexander was now a wealthy man and the whole world lay open before him. But where should he go? To the South Sea like his friend, Georg Forster? To the Caribbean islands, Siberia, Africa, or perhaps to the Americas? For the time being, Alexander postponed his decision and first went about collecting all of the necessary instruments he would need for his scientific research: thermometers and barometers for measuring temperature and atmospheric pressure. Microscopes for studying plants and insects in detail. Telescopes for stargazing. Compasses and sextants for navigating.

With this valuable cargo, Alexander made his way to Italy and Switzerland to test out the instruments and to conduct studies in botany, zoology, geology, and astronomy. In wind, rain, or snow—in every kind of weather, Alexander was outside exploring. At the same time, he was constantly reading about other explorers' travels, books about the latest scientific studies, and exchanging letters with the most respected scholars of his time. At last, he felt he was well-enough prepared for his first long journey.

"Few travelers have had to overcome as many difficulties as those that I faced before departing for the Spanish Americas."

In the meantime, all of Europe was in upheaval. In 1789, the people of France rebelled against their king and, with cries of "freedom, equality, and fraternity!" opened the path toward a new era. Alexander was enthusiastic about these progressive ideas. But the dream of better times for all people was sadly not to be. In 1804, Napoleon was crowned emperor and immediately set out to conquer Europe. The great nations went to war: England, Prussia, Austria-Hungary, Spain, and France fought against each other—on land and at sea. It was hardly a good time to venture out into the world.

NAPOLEON

In 1789, the French people overthrew their king and got rid of the monarchy. Then the nation plunged into chaos. A general named Napoleon Bonaparte seized the opportunity. He was crowned emperor in 1804 after promising peace and order. But instead he promptly sent his troops to wage endless wars. His armies conquered half of Europe but finally lost the Battle of Waterloo in 1815 against England and Prussia. The emperor was overthrown and banished.

With all of Europe at war, Alexander was surprised to learn about a French expedition led by Captain Nicolas Baudin, who intended to leave for the Antarctic soon. Alexander set off at once for Paris in the hopes of catching the captain before it was too late. But shortly after arriving, he heard that the expedition had been canceled for lack of funds. Next, he heard about an expedition to North Africa that was leaving from the port city of Marseille in South France. *Then that's where I will go,* Alexander said to himself. This would not be the only time that he would hastily change his travel plans, but he did not yet know it.

This time, Alexander was not going by himself. In Paris, he had met a young French scientist staying in the same house. His name was Aimé Bonpland. The young doctor served in the French marines but was far more interested in the study of plants. He, too, wanted to travel the world. So, it was no great surprise that the two young men became quick friends. "We are going to be a good team," said Alexander. "But I don't have any money," said the Frenchman sadly. "No problem," Alexander told him, "I will cover the cost." Aimé agreed and packed his things. The only uncertainty now was when they would be able to leave.

But this was the start of an unusual friendship. Alexander was a disciplined man who concentrated fully on his work and scientific studies.

Aimé, by contrast, liked to pursue the other joys of life: He frequently enjoyed a glass of wine and kept an eye out for girls. Whereas Alexander was restless and could hardly sleep at night, Aimé was very good at sitting relaxed in the sunshine. Because of these differences, the two men would often get into big fights, though it would never destroy their friendship.

For the time being, however, the two men were stuck in Marseille because they couldn't find the expedition ship. Finally, they learned that the ship was not going to come because it had been heavily damaged in a storm. Foiled again! Still, Alexander remained hopeful. "Let's go to Spain," he told his partner. "Perhaps we'll have more luck there."

As they traveled, Alexander continued testing out his instruments. He measured the height of mountains and the width of rivers, assessed temperatures and humidity. Aimé spent time collecting herbs and flowers that he didn't recognize from his own country. They both kept meticulous notes on everything. Finally, the two young men arrived in Madrid, the Spanish capital city from which King Carlos IV ruled over a vast empire.

> **"No other foreigner had ever been honored with as much trust from the Spanish government."**

Spain controlled colonies in Asia and on the South American continent. The Spanish didn't like foreigners travelling through the realm for fear they might be spies. Putting all his skills of persuasion and inspiration to work, Alexander successfully gained the trust of King Carlos. He promised to bring back exotic plants for the royal gardens in Madrid. Because of his experience in mining, he also agreed to help the Spanish in their efforts to mine gold and silver in South America and Mexico.

Once Alexander explained his intention to pay for the voyage himself, the king was convinced. He issued the companions passports to all of the colonies. The authorities in every Spanish American region were commanded to graciously receive the two men and offer them anything they needed. They would even be allowed to sail on Spanish ships if necessary. In this way, they became the very first foreigners allowed to roam freely throughout the Spanish colonies.

The year was 1799. Alexander was thirty years old as he, together with Aimé Bonpland, boarded the postal ship *Pizarro*, which set sail from the Spanish harbor city of La Coruña. The destination was the Caribbean island of Cuba. More than forty instruments had been packed into wooden crates, as well as tools, writing paper, and containers for collecting minerals, seeds, flowers, and soil samples. At last, the long-awaited expedition could begin.

The volcano of Tenerife

Crossing the Atlantic Ocean, most ships stopped at the Canary Islands, which was also under the rule of the Spanish Empire. The *Pizarro* was no exception. Naturally, Alexander stood at the ship's railing with his telescope as they sailed closer to the island. "There's nothing to see. Too much fog," he said sadly to the captain. "Just wait," the captain replied. And then, after a short while, the fog suddenly broke open and the island of Tenerife rose before them with its volcano Pico del Teide.

A dragon tree can grow up to 70 feet high.

The first early-morning sunbeams unveiled a visual feast for the eyes: the light first illuminating the mountaintop and then slowly meandering downward toward the coast. "We simply must climb that mountain," Alexander declared. The captain agreed to a short stopover. "But don't take too long," he urged. "We have a long journey ahead of us to America."

Alexander and Aimé needed to be quick. They tried to find a local guide on the island who would take them up the mountain. But among the indigenous peoples, it appeared no one had ever climbed the volcano. The mountain was 12,198 feet high, the highest in all of Spain. Its slopes were craggy and scalding air bubbled up from its surface in places.

"Why would you want to go up there?" the people asked. "There's nothing but cliffs, snow, and fumes that stink like rotten eggs. You won't find anything up there that you can bring back, not even water." Some of them believed the crater of the volcano was the entrance to the underworld, controlled by dark spirits.

Eventually, they were able to hire a few porters who agreed to carry their heavy instruments to the top in exchange for good pay. As they climbed, Aimé inspected every plant, sometimes picking one and bringing it along. He had never seen anything like them, not even during his biology studies. In fact, some of the plants could only be found on the Canary Islands. Aimé was particularly impressed by the palm trees and banana plants that he now saw for the first time in their native habitat. The indigenous porters were confused and wondered how anyone could be amazed by something so ordinary, but they didn't say anything.

FIRE FROM INSIDE THE EARTH

Enormous pressure and heat cause stone within the earth's belly to melt. We call this fiery liquid magma. It oozes out wherever there are cracks and holes in the earth's crust. Sometimes this happens slowly and a glowing stream of molten rock called lava pours out of the earth. As the air cools the lava bit by bit, a cone-shaped mountain is formed: a volcano. If the pressure inside the earth becomes extreme, there is an explosion of gases, ash, and huge boulders that burst out of the crater and fly hundreds of feet into the air.

But every time Alexander stopped and tried to examine and collect various rocks, the porters got irritated. "Why should we have to carry those heavy things all around?" they asked. The two explorers pressed and encouraged them to keep going, but only the promised payment spurred them onward.

The group climbed higher and higher. Now there were only a few occasional goats and rabbits on the slopes. From the outset of their hike at sea level, where tropical plants grew lush and green, the men had moved through zone after zone of changing vegetation. They soon crossed into a variety of forest they recognized from Europe. "It's as if we've traveled from the equator to the north pole," Alexander said to his friend.

"The higher we go, the cooler the temperature and the sparser the vegetation." The vegetation soon disappeared altogether, and even the most rugged plants could no longer survive in the cold and harsh winds. The wanderers stumbled across loose scree and their going became much slower. Their steps stirred up dust that followed them. Every now and then they crossed a lava flow: liquid rock from a volcanic eruption that had been pushed out from the inside of the earth and had now cooled down. The sharp edges of the lava cut into the soles of their boots.

Soon night fell and darkness descended. They spent the night outside, but they had not brought along warm coats or tents. Even though it was high summer and they were at the edge of the tropics, the temperatures dropped dangerously low. "It's only forty degrees Fahrenheit," Alexander read from his thermometer. The porters grumbled.

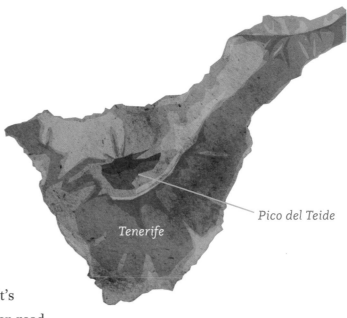

Pico del Teide

Tenerife

By 3:00 AM the next morning, the party was already off with torches to light the way. One of the porters fell and smashed the water bottles. But going back was not an option for Alexander. They had almost reached the snow line. At the top of the peak, the Pico del Teide summit was covered in snow. The valley and coastline were no longer visible; the hikers had climbed higher than the clouds that had rolled in again overnight. The cloud layer spread out below them like a white, wooly sea.

At last, they reached the summit, which was covered with volcanic ash and debris. The clouds had retreated and now the climbers could gaze out across the entire island at their feet: the inhabited towns and fields and then—as though tier by tier—the various vegetation zones. Tenerife looked like one single immense mountain rising up from the wide ocean. They could see the other Canary Islands floating on the horizon: Gran Canaria, Lanzarote, Fuerteventura, La Palma, and La Gomera. "Fantastic!" Aimé exclaimed, unable to tear his gaze away from the sea and sky. *My very first volcano,* Alexander thought to himself, captivated. It would not be his last.

Alexander's thirst for knowledge soon had him pushing the limits. His porters were furious when they saw he was now climbing down into the crater

"We could not get enough of the azure-hued sky from the peak of the volcano."

Humboldt used a cyanometer like this during his travels to measure the blue of the sky.

of the volcano. Alexander wanted to see everything up close, and since he had
already come this far, how could he say no to one final small detour?

An icy wind swirled and made him freeze in spite of the sun overhead. In some spots, steam hissed out between fissures, so scorching hot that he had to stay away to keep from burning his skin. Alexander collected more rocks and even used a bottle to scoop up some air that he would later be able to study chemically from the ship.

It was high time to hurry back down to the plains. The descent was as harrowing as the climb because the men slid and fell constantly on the loose ash. To make the going easier, the porters threw away many of the rocks that Alexander had spent so much time collecting. But he only saw what they were doing after it was too late.

When they got close to the harbor, Alexander and Aimé were shocked to see that their ship had already unfurled its sail. They dashed on board just as the captain gave the order to depart. "We have to leave," he said. "It's a favorable wind and we have a long journey ahead of us."

Across the Atlantic

For the first time in his life, Alexander was sailing across the great ocean between Africa and America. For three straight weeks they sailed on open water with no land in sight. The seabirds from the Canary Islands flew alongside the ship for a few days as it left the island, but then they turned around. The sea was calm and the temperatures were warm and comfortable in the day and at night. The wind blew the ship at a steady speed so the sailors hardly had to work. "It's almost as if we were sailing down a river," Alexander observed, recalling the choppy waves of the North Sea from his trip to England. "Yes," the captain replied, "that's why almost every Spanish ship has taken this same route to America for the last three hundred years." On their return, they would have to take another route farther north, where the seas were stormier. But Alexander didn't want to think about that now. He was much too excited about their next stop.

The journey thus far had already proved thrilling. He regularly took down the temperature of the air and water and measured the humidity and ocean currents. As was his habit, he wrote down all the information in his notebook. The sailors whispered anxiously among themselves about a dangerous maelstrom, a swirling ocean current that can drag ships to the bottom of the sea. Alexander measured the movements of the waves and ocean more often but he couldn't detect any signs of approaching danger. The ocean appeared as calm as ever. "It's nothing but the sailors' imagination and superstition," he wrote in his notes.

One morning, Alexander stood at the ship railing when he suddenly could not believe his eyes. Flying fish shot ten to fifteen feet up out of the water. Some of the fish were caught by large seabirds; others fell and landed on the deck of the ship. Naturally, Alexander had to get a closer look at these strange ocean dwellers. He discovered that they had an extra-large swim bladder filled with air. This made them lighter than other fish and allowed them to catapult themselves effortlessly out of the water.

The most beautiful time was at night. The farther the ship sailed to the south, the more dramatically the stars shifted in the sky. Familiar constellations disappeared and new ones took their place. The sea air was especially crisp and clean, making the stars appear all the more brilliant.

For the first time in his life, Alexander saw the southern cross that his friend Georg Forster had spoken about so often. One of his boyhood dreams was thus fulfilled. The sailors on board the *Pizarro* had often seen the constellation; for them, it was like an old friend. But even they were happy at the sight

"In the solitude of the sea, one greets a star like a friend."

THE CONSTELLATION OF LONGING

The night sky of the southern hemisphere is different from that of the north because you are looking into the universe from a different angle. The most well known constellation is the Southern Cross. The early seafarers used it to navigate across the ocean because it helps to determine a southern direction. The Southern Cross is not visible from the northern hemisphere, which is why it is often a symbol of wanderlust and a yearning to visit the tropics.

because it reminded them that they would soon reach the coast, where they could disembark onto the sunny beaches of the Caribbean island of Cuba.

As the ship neared the American continent, the dangers of a sea voyage seemed to have passed. But then a sudden illness and fever broke out among some of those on board. The air below deck in the cabins was hot and oppressive. "The people don't have fresh air," wrote Alexander, who had spent the majority of the trip up on deck. The ship lacked effective medicines, and so the contagious fever spread among the passengers. The ill had to be brought to a hospital on land as soon as possible.

TRADE WINDS

At the end of the eighteenth century, ships did not have any motors. They used sails to move and were thus reliant on good winds. In crossing the Atlantic Ocean, sailors made good use of trade winds, which reliably blew from Europe directly to the Americas.

The captain decided to skip Cuba for the time being. Instead, he wanted to reach the next available coastline. But where was it? The nautical charts in those days were imprecise, some of them downright false. The Spanish, French, and English charts on board contradicted each other.

Using his instruments, Alexander was able to determine the current location of the ship. "New Andalucia Province and the port of Cumaná are not far off," Alexander informed the captain, pointing. But the captain preferred to trust his own instincts and experience. He laughed at Alexander's prediction that they were close to the coast of South America. But Alexander was right. Forty-one days after their departure from La Coruña, the mountains of New Andalucia Province, what is known today as Venezuela, appeared through the mist.

As they pushed in toward land, they could see the coconut trees swaying in the wind along the beach of Cumaná. The tropical sun was blazing and the air was scorching hot. Pelicans, herons, and flamingos flapped in the breeze and were the first to greet those on board from a totally new, totally foreign world. Alexander and Aimé had managed to evade the fever, but they decided not to continue on to Cuba with the *Pizarro*. The risk of contracting the illness was still high. "Another change of plans," Alexander reported, "but we're getting used to it by now."

"The nature in these climates seems more active, more fruitful, one might even say, more lavish with life."

Chapter 3

Venezuela
First steps in South America

Meanwhile, Alexander and Aimé had become good friends. From their very first step onto the beaches of Cumaná, they were awestruck. "So many strange trees, shrubs, and flowers," marveled Aimé, even though he was a botanist and therefore already familiar with many plant varieties. But here, everything was new and different.

It was a wonderland of glorious colors bursting at the shoots. All of the proportions were gigantic: huge mountains, huge rivers, huge vegetation. The nature was so wild and overgrown it was a struggle for the explorers just to push through the undergrowth. Never before had the two travelers seen anything like it.

For the time being, they took up lodging in the port city of Cumaná. From here, they set out every day in spite of the sweltering heat to explore the surrounding region. They walked along beaches, where the feather-like branches of palm trees protruded against the blue sky and rustled in the wind. They climbed up hills and mountains, where they had to keep an eye out for rattlesnakes. Prickly cacti grew close together, forming an impenetrable wall. The two men canoed up rivers where dolphins and crocodiles were swimming. Above their heads flew pelicans, herons, albatross, vultures, enormous flocks of colorful parrots, and swarms of butterflies. They went inside caves where thousands of night birds built their nests.

When twilight fell, they observed and measured the starry sky. The constellations were different here than they had been on the voyage at sea. They watched shooting stars streak across the inky blackness. And they were delighted by the millions of fireflies that fluttered around them.

But their favorite thing to do was to venture deep into the rain forest. It was here that wild nature popped at the seams and had gone topsy-turvy, with roots tangled in a jumble. Giant trees were so covered in moss, orchids, and climbing vines that one could hardly see them in spite of their size. Canes of bamboo and heavy ferns made it nearly impossible to proceed. The tree canopy overhead was so dense that the light remained dim all day long. The explorers couldn't even see a speck of sky. Aimé was frustrated by all the plants he could not reach. How could he get up to the leaves, blossoms, and fruits of the trees when the lowest branches were sixty feet off the ground?

Alexander and Aimé began to get used to the heat. They even started to "freeze" like the locals every time the thermometer dipped below 70 degrees. But Aimé was rattled by the powerful booming thunderstorms that rolled in every afternoon. The loud storms unleashed an outpouring of rain for two-hour stretches, but the cool air that accompanied the storms did not last for long. The air soon turned sticky and humid again. "You'll just have to get used to it," Alexander told him. "It's like that for months in the tropics."

"One becomes accustomed to the notion of a world that feeds only plants and animals, and in which the ringing and bellows of human joys and sorrows never sound at all."

The people of Cumaná were curious about the foreigners' excursions. They themselves didn't like to venture much farther than a stroll along the boardwalk. They enjoyed cooling off in the river when it was hot. In the evenings, adults dragged their chairs out into the water and sat chatting until long into the night. The children spent much of their lives in the water.

Alexander's instruments aroused the interest of the locals. Why was the foreigner always measuring everything, especially if he didn't even own the land or plan to buy it? Was he looking for gold? They simply could not believe that anyone would travel so far just to collect plants and look at the stars. They were amazed by someone who would not only enjoy nature or figure out how to exploit it but also wanted to understand how it works. "I want to know how each of the numerous individual parts of our Earth fit together. I wish to comprehend how the climate and the seasons influence the lives of animals and plants," Alexander explained to

THE TROPICS

The tropics can be found on both sides of the equator, in the north and in the south. Depending on the elevation and season, these regions may contain lush rain forests, dry savannahs, or snow-covered mountains. Venezuela is one of the few countries where all three of these landscapes are found together.

his hosts. But his hosts did not particularly care and had already started eating their dinner and complaining once again about the heat.

As much as Alexander was delighted by the wildlife of this strange world, he was furious about what took place at the Cumaná marketplace. Every day, slaves were bought and sold there. Alexander did not agree with such a trade. The black Africans had first been brutally captured on their native soil and then forced onto ships and brought to the Americas. Anyone who had survived the perilous journey across the Atlantic was sold in the marketplaces to rich landowners, where they were then forced to work for twelve or more hours at a time in the hot fields.

Alexander was outraged over such treatment of fellow human beings, but as a guest in this land he felt there was little he could do. All his life he would remember these poor people. He would never waste a chance to protest this form of human exploitation.

Throughout their travels, Alexander and Aimé came across various Catholic missions erected by Spanish monks scattered across the colonial kingdom. The monks intended to convert the indigenous peoples to the Christian faith of European culture. To that end, they had created small settlements in the jungles, built houses, and established local farming practices. A charitable example of Christian neighborly love, one might think. However, the indigenous people didn't seem very happy to Alexander. It seemed like they would rather be free to live on their own in the jungle, perhaps to hunt and gather as they had done before.

One day, Alexander and Aimé experienced their first earthquake. It wasn't a very strong one but it was enough to frighten them both. A powerful jolt shook the bedrock deep underground. The solid foundation of the earth was apparently much less solid than they had supposed. While Aimé trembled with fear, Alexander had already recovered and was pulling out his instruments quickly to start measuring temperature, humidity, and magnetism. He scrupulously wrote down any observable effects of the earthquake.

For the rest of their long journey through other parts of the Americas, the two men would experience more earthquakes and they would eventually get used to it. Soon they would view earthquakes as no more alarming than a familiar boom of thunder. At night, they learned to stay put in bed whenever the underground layers started to rumble and the surface of the earth began to shake. But they were lucky; they never had to experience the kind of devastating earthquake that can easily destroy an entire city.

> "For the first time, you become wary of the ground on which you have been walking for a long time."

EARTHQUAKES
Our Earth is composed of gigantic stone plates that are slowly moving in all different directions. In some places, they bump up against each other, push up on top or below, or press together with enormous force. When the pressure gets to be too much, there is a tremendous jolt from inside the earth. The shock ripples out to the surface of the earth, where the ground trembles and shakes.

Alexander had been pondering an idea for quite some time, but now he decided to share it with his friend: Before sailing on to Cuba, he wanted to get away from the coast and go deep into the Venezuelan interior. "Haven't we had our fill of adventures here?" Aimé asked. "Of course not," exclaimed Alexander, "there's still so much to discover! Besides, there is a great puzzle we still need to solve." "What kind of puzzle?" Aimé pressed. But Alexander decided to keep it a secret for now. "I'll tell you later," he said. And so, the companions set off on the next phase of their journey—into the mysterious heart of South America.

A waterway through the jungle

A hair hygrometer to measure humidity

With a tinge of sadness, Alexander and Aimé left Cumaná. They had only stayed there for five months, but it already felt like home. After all, this was the place where they had taken their very first steps on an unfamiliar continent. For the rest of his life, Alexander would always look back wistfully on the trip to this part of Venezuela. However, now it was time to leave.

Their goal was to reach the great Orinoco River that flows through the northern part of South America. The river passage was their only chance to be able to get through the otherwise impassable jungle in the middle of the continent. But in order to get there, they would first have to cross los Llanos, a vast grassy stretch of plains without trees or shrubs. It was so flat and monotonous that it looked like an ocean. Only rarely did the shadow of a tiny cloud appear. In the dry season, the ground cracked and the grass withered to dust.

Crossing los Llanos was an enormous undertaking for everyone—people, horses, and mules. They needed water and supplies for four weeks to be able to survive in the barren landscape. In addition, Alexander and Aimé had the difficult task of transporting all their tools and instruments in the sweltering heat.

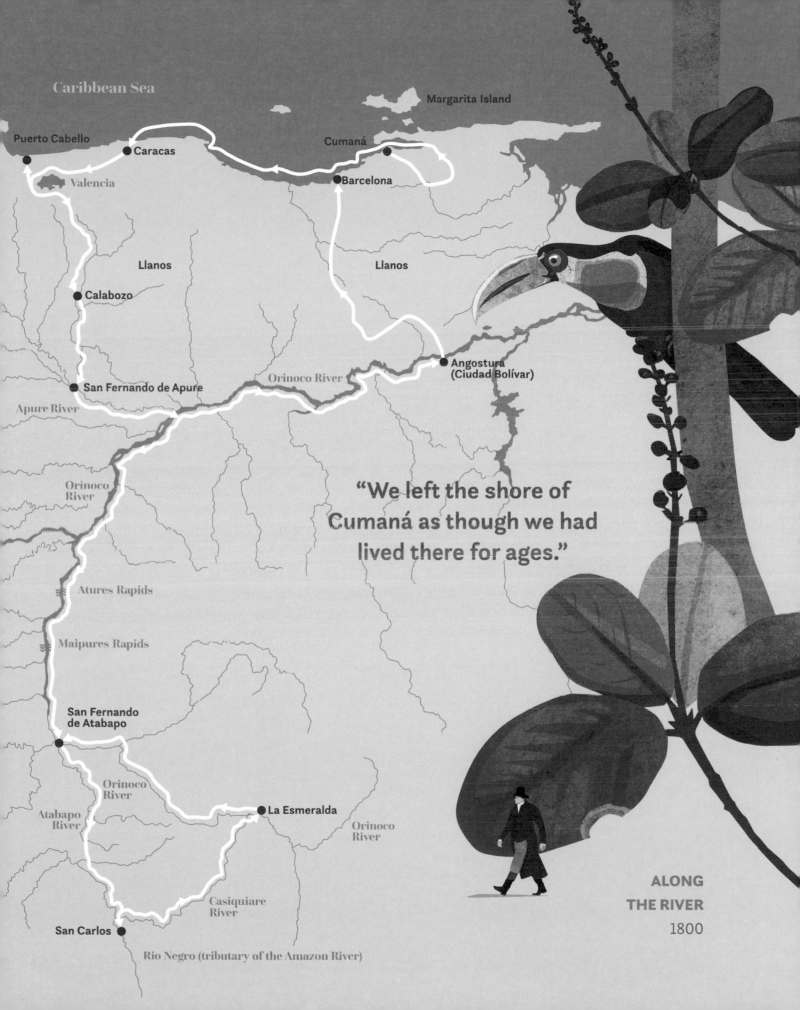

Caribbean Sea

Margarita Island

Puerto Cabello

Caracas

Valencia

Cumaná

Barcelona

Llanos

Llanos

Calabozo

Angostura
(Ciudad Bolívar)

San Fernando de Apure

Orinoco River

Apure River

Orinoco
River

Atures Rapids

Maipures Rapids

"We left the shore of
Cumaná as though we had
lived there for ages."

San Fernando
de Atabapo

Orinoco
River

Atabapo
River

La Esmeralda

Orinoco
River

Casiquiare
River

San Carlos

ALONG

THE RIVER

1800

Rio Negro (tributary of the Amazon River)

They had to protect them from the dust and sandstorms that were constantly sweeping across the flat plains.

Fortunately, Alexander had been able to send the rocks and plants he had already gathered back to Europe. A trusted acquaintance had taken them from Cumaná. Now they had space for collecting new specimens. In the coming days, however, there was nothing to see but dry grass. Because of the blazing sun, they traveled mostly at night. Sometimes they passed a small pond or tiny stream. They longed to dive in and take a refreshing bath. But, their guides warned them: Crocodiles!

They soon encountered another strange animal in the waters: the electric eel. Whoever touched it was in for a big shock! That such a creature could exist was hard to believe, so of course Alexander didn't shy away from the chance to examine it more thoroughly. And what he discovered was that the eel truly *did* emit strong enough electrical surges to harm a horse. "This is indeed a living electrical apparatus," Alexander marveled.

In spite of their difficult journey, he was fascinated by this landscape. The absence of hills or mountains gave the travelers an unlimited view in every direction. "Maybe it's bleak and boring," he said to Aimé, "but I just love this endless horizon." The world appeared to stretch on for eternity.

The landscape and climate slowly began to change. The rainy season kicked off with a terrific thunderstorm. The vegetation became more lush and now and then trees started to appear along their route. The travelers had finally reached the rain forest and a tributary of the great Orinoco River. In a small village, they encountered a few monks who had not crossed paths with other Europeans for a very long time.

The next thing to do was locate a very large canoe. Alexander and Aimé had to be sure their valuable instruments were tightly secured on the wobbly boat. They would also need to bulk up on supplies for the next few weeks: flour, bananas, cocoa, and even a couple of live hens for eggs. They didn't know if they would have a chance to hunt or fish along the way. What lay ahead was a great mystery. White people had scarcely ever set foot in these parts before. Sometimes they would come across a tiny mission outpost where someone could understand their language.

But they couldn't find any indigenous guides who completely knew the way they wanted to go. And no one had ever drawn any trustworthy maps of the region. This would prove to be Alexander's most important task. It was a good thing that he was such a talented and studied artist. He had always enjoyed drawing from a young age and had had the best art teacher he could wish for, Daniel Chodowiecki, a famous etcher.

Traveling to the river was much more exciting than crossing the plains of Los Llanos. But it was also more dangerous. Countless crocodiles dozed on the banks of the river or swam in its current. Gigantic snakes slept on trees or wriggled through the water. Jaguars prowled through the jungle. The uprooted trunks of gigantic trees bobbed along in the river, threatening to crush the canoe.

Slowly, the two adventurers grew bolder. While one would wash off in the river, the other kept watch for danger. It worked. Alexander often sipped the river water and took note of the different tastes. At last, they reached the main artery of the Orinoco River.

From here, the journey took a more difficult turn, as they now had to travel upstream. Every time the wind was unfavorable, the indigenous guides had to paddle against the current. Sometimes they swam to shore and pulled the boat along with a rope. The river was violent and reminded them of the sea. In some places, Alexander measured that the river was three miles wide. Most of the time they couldn't go far from the riverbanks because an impenetrable jumble of trees, bushes, and climbing vines formed a thick, green barrier. But

"We were not unmoved to encounter
for the first time the long-awaited
waters of the Orinoco."

behind the barrier was a colorful, wildly profuse habitat unlike any other in the world. Countless plants and animals, thousands of unknown species vying for life. Devouring each other and being devoured. This was nature in its wildest, most untamed form. Here humans were not in control but were only a single tiny, completely insignificant part of the natural order. "The jungle does not pay attention to us," Alexander remarked.

"Perhaps it does," Aimé argued later, when they were swarmed by mosquitoes on every side and at every minute of the day. The mosquitoes were a terrible nuisance. "There are more mosquitoes here than air," the indigenous guides even complained. The insects crawled into their eyes and noses and bit them through their clothing. After only a few days, all of the men were covered with too many mosquito bites to count. The itching was so awful they could hardly sleep. At least lemon and pineapple juice helped to soothe it somewhat.

Eventually, the men got used to the mosquitoes. But then they were awakened at night when the jaguars went hunting and all the other jungle animals started sending out warning signals in the form of whoops and loud shrieks. When that would happen, the entire jungle crescendoed into a noisy uproar.

Solving a geographical puzzle

The wide Orinoco River flowed lethargically through the jungle. But at some point upstream, the river was wedged between two mountain ranges, and there the travelers found their way blocked by a series of dangerous rapids and waterfalls: the Atures and Maipures Rapids. For several miles, the river plunged steeply down stone steps, boulders, and cliffs. "It looks like a sea of foam!" Alexander shouted enthusiastically.

Although the sight of such towering waterfalls was magnificent, it also posed a few problems. The canoe had to be unloaded and each piece of luggage laboriously carried up along the banks. Whenever possible, the men towed the boat

through the whirling waters on a rope. But in some places they had no choice but to pull it out of the water and carry it on land. The complications delayed the journey by three days until the whole expedition had made it to the top of the waterfall. But there was at least one benefit: Because neither crocodiles nor snakes swam in the rapids, the travelers were at last free to bathe in peace.

Alexander, ever the inquisitive explorer, began to consider how the river might be diverted to create a canal. This would allow ships to easily bypass the waterfall. He had already concocted a plan in his head. He later suggested the idea to the governor of Venezuela, but no one has ever undertaken such a venture.

None of the difficulties of their journey could discourage the two travelers from their work. Day and night, Alexander and Aimé kept their ears and eyes peeled to their surroundings. Alexander constantly measured the temperature

of the air and water, and he tried to figure out their precise geographical locations. They had soon collected a small zoo of beetles, birds, and monkeys. Aimé gathered as many plants as he could. And yet, he was constantly mumbling to himself "Too bad, too bad," because the most beautiful and colorful specimens of flowers and leaves were out of his reach far overhead in the tree canopy.

The constant twitter of birds they could not see and the howling of unseen monkeys swinging through the jungle followed them wherever they went. The two researchers longed to take a closer look. But it was important not to get *too* close to these jungle creatures. Alexander experienced this one day as they were walking along the riverbanks. He suddenly came face-to-face with a jaguar. He was able to recall what the indigenous guides had instructed him and made a slow and cautious retreat. Don't look back! Luck once again favored the adventurer.

It was soon time for Alexander and Aimé to try solving a wondrous geographical puzzle: There were rumors that the two great rivers of South America—the Orinoco and the Amazon—were linked by a natural canal. If this was true, boats would be able to cross the continent from Venezuela to Brazil. Several Spanish missionaries claimed to have seen and used such a water passage. They called it Casiquiare. But everyone had drawn a different map, which was confusing because of the multiple rivers that snaked through the jungles. A lot of Europeans doubted reports of the river link, dismissing it as geographical nonsense. "That would be like saying the Rhine and the Danube Rivers have a natural connection," the scholars mocked.

But Alexander had another opinion. "Why shouldn't things be different here than they are in our old, familiar world?" he asked himself and his travel companion, Aimé. His friend was not very interested. But, of course, he went along on Alexander's search for Casiquiare. He had unfortunately lost some of his collection of plants from small canoe mishaps over the previous weeks. He leaped at the chance to find more plants for his botany collection.

On and on they paddled upstream through the maze of jungle rivers. At last they came to what had to be the Casiquiare. "This is no canal," Alexander observed, "this is a part of the Orinoco." The large river apparently divided at La Esmeralda, flowing eastward as the Orinoco River toward Venezuela and south as the Casiquiare toward the Amazon River in Brazil. Alexander determined the exact location of the fork in the river. And he drew up the first truly accurate map of the link between the Orinoco and Amazon Rivers.

CHRISTOPHER COLUMBUS

The Italian explorer, under service to the Spanish crown, reached the Americas but didn't even realize it, as he was looking for a sea passage to Asia. When he reached land after sailing for weeks in 1492, he thought it was the east coast of India. Only after he died was it clear that he had landed on continents previously unknown to Europeans: the Americas.

"When the Spanish kingdom learns of this, they will set up a great trade route here," Alexander predicted. Such a water passage would allow for the transport of goods from the north part of South America to the center of the continent and back. Soon, Alexander believed, a great city would be constructed at this fork in the river. But he was wrong. The area was too remote and too inhospitable with its climate and mosquitoes to build a city. Even today, more than two hundred years after Alexander von Humboldt's journey, this part of Venezuela remains nearly untouched in the middle of the rain forest.

Alexander and Aimé were now faced with a choice: Should they go right along the Orinoco arm of the river, back toward their starting point on the coast of Venezuela? Or should they follow the left arm, the Casiquiare, on to further uncharted paths in Brazil? They decided to turn back to the more familiar course. Doing so would allow them to take their collections and notes safely back to the coast and send them on to Europe.

THE SPANISH COLONIAL KINGDOM

Soon after Columbus's voyage, the Spanish Empire set about to conquer the new continent. In the search for gold and silver, they battled one indigenous tribe after another. In time, they controlled almost the entire region from Alaska to Chile. It wasn't until the start of the nineteenth century that the colonies began to break from Spanish rule. After suffering through years of cruelty, subjugation, and misrule, many countries that we know today declared independence from their colonizers: from Mexico to Chile, and Cuba to Argentina.

Traveling downstream on the river went much faster now. The current pulled them along and most of the time they didn't even need to paddle. Finally, they arrived in the provincial capital of Angostura, which today is called Ciudad Bolívar.

They had been canoeing on Venezuela's rivers for nearly three months and had covered more than 1,200 miles. Now they could once again sleep with a roof over their heads. Alexander and Aimé were delighted by even the simplest comforts of civilization. A dry bed and a fresh piece of bread felt miraculous to them both.

Oddly enough, now of all times, after having survived the worst hardships, Aimé fell ill. His high fever puzzled the doctors. Had he contracted something on their detour to the Casiquiare River? Was he going to die? Alexander felt bad about pushing his friend to go so far with him. But Aimé did not lose heart and even managed to stay cheerful. The illness lasted for six weeks, but eventually Aimé felt better. Now they were free to return to the coast.

To get there, they had to cross los Llanos once again, the seemingly endless plains. But this time they hardly recognized it. The plains were no longer parched but rather overflowing after the rainy season. There were gigantic lakes and wide rivers where only four months ago there was nothing but flat grassland. There were also several different kinds of animals now. "This confirms one of the basic laws of nature," Alexander told his friend. "When one important element changes, it affects all the other components of the plant and animal world." One thing had stayed the same, however, Aimé replied: the unhindered view. "Finally, a wide-open vista in every direction!"

"Basic houses looked splendid to us now, and everyone we spoke with seemed witty."

Arriving at the coast, Alexander and Aimé had to wait a few more weeks to find a ship that was willing to take them along. They had been in Venezuela for sixteen months and now they wanted to travel via Cuba and Mexico to the Philippines. However, this plan, like so many others the companions had made before, would prove to be as fleeting as the wind.

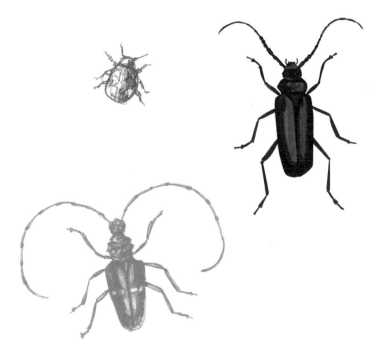

Chapter 4

THROUGH THE ANDES MOUNTAINS
From the swelter to cooler climes

Alexander and Aimé had hardly set foot in the Cuban capital when they learned about a French expedition returning to South America on its way toward Australia. This would be their chance to travel around the globe. "We simply must go," Alexander said. "Do you think they'll even consider taking us along?" his companion asked. "And how can we find the expedition?" These were all good questions of course, but Alexander wasn't worried. "We'll travel along the coast of Peru toward Lima. Surely we'll catch up with the French explorers there." Aimé was once again caught up in his friend's enthusiasm for adventure.

It was impractical for the two men to bring their collections or notes along on this uncertain detour. They put some of their objects on a ship headed to England, others on a ship to France, and decided to store the remaining collection in Cuba for the time being. This way, if anything was lost at sea, they would still have everything else.

With ease of mind, the adventurers had set off toward Peru. But unfortunately, a few weeks later they learned that the French expedition had actually set out in the opposite direction and would not be visiting Lima at all. By then,

Alexander and Aimé were back on the northern coast of South America, this time in the port city of Cartagena. They were in Colombia, which in those days the Spanish called New Granada. What should they do now?

"Let's change our plans completely and go explore the Andes Mountains," Alexander insisted. Aimé had gotten used to his friend's frequent change of plans by now. "OK, why not," he agreed. After all, the Andes are the longest mountain chain in the world—stretching approximately 4,500 miles from the Caribbean coast to Tierra del Fuego. Aimé was certain to discover more new plant varieties along the way.

EL DORADO

The Spanish Empire ruthlessly exploited their colonies. They were particularly avid in the hunt for gold. Even after they stole all the gold they could find from the indigenous Inca and Aztec peoples, they still wanted more. They searched feverishly for El Dorado, a legendary land of gold brimming with riches—of course without success. But their greed led them farther, into the Andes between Colombia and Peru and deep into the jungles of Venezuela and Bolivia. They never found it.

In order to get from the coast to the mountains, Alexander and Aimé first had to paddle up the large Magdalena River in a canoe. This time they knew what to expect: two months surrounded by nothing but jungle, suffocating heat, crocodiles, and, of course, inescapable swarms of hungry mosquitoes.

By the time they reached the mountains, the travelers were relieved to finally emerge from the terrible conditions. But their path ahead would not be much easier. Now began the constant upward march on small, craggy paths. Their way brought them up through narrow, muggy ravines used by Inca warriors hundreds of years ago. Whereas those warriors had been tough climbers used to difficult conditions, Alexander and Aimé had hardly stretched their muscles for months after traveling on ships and sitting in the canoe.

The nights were icy cold. The higher Alexander and Aimé climbed, the less oxygen was available. Breathing was difficult and they began to get headaches. Slowly, they adjusted to the thin air, and when they did, they realized it wasn't such an inhabitable place after all. In fact, there were lots of people living and thriving at these elevations high in the mountains.

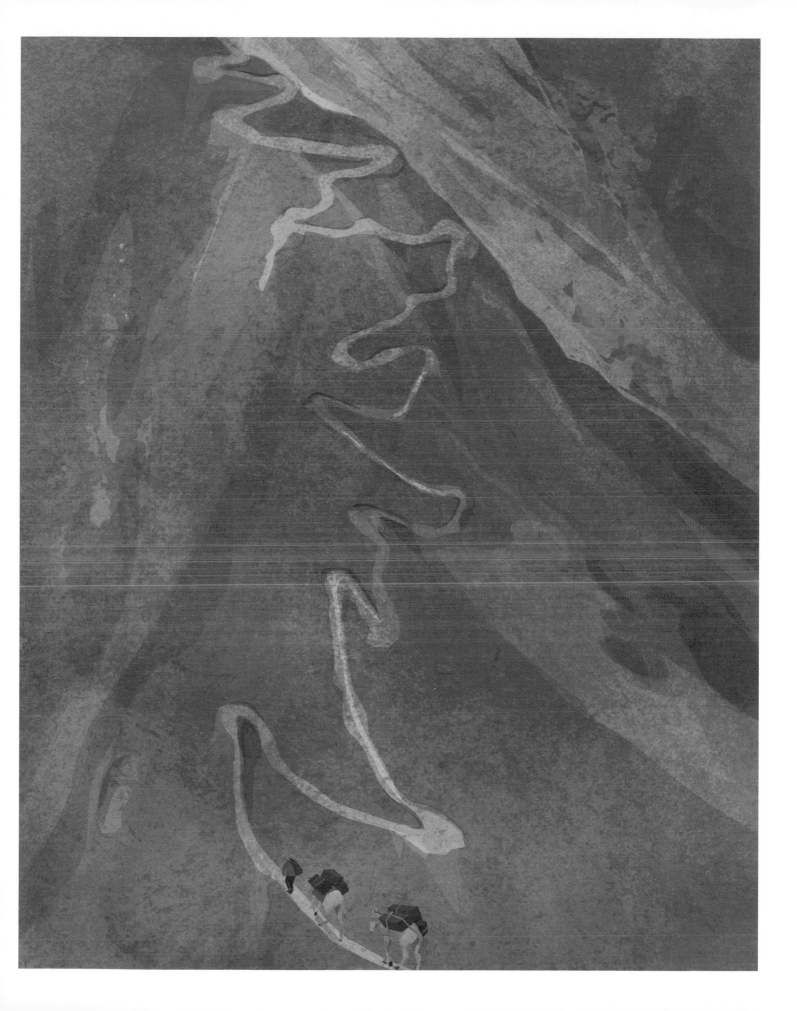

Bogotá

SIMÓN BOLÍVAR

Two decades after Humboldt's visit to Bogotá, the city became the main headquarters for General Simón Bolívar. The general had met Humboldt in Paris years earlier and discussed the region of South America. Now he was demanding independence of the entire continent from Spanish rule. He fought so successfully against Spain with his troops that he did in fact gain independence for many parts of the continent.

The colonial city of Bogotá, which the friends soon reached, was a good example of one such bustling, high-altitude city. Located at 8,660 feet above sea level, today the city is the capital of Colombia. Life was pleasant at such heights and the inhabitants of the city loved to hold festivals and celebrations. Many of the locals had read about the Baron von Humboldt in Spanish newspapers that had been reporting on Alexander's South American expedition. Alexander and Aimé thus received a warm welcome and were invited to stay with a prominent family. Of course, they were asked to tell their travel stories. The locals were amazed at the friends' tales of peril and adventure and at times did not even believe them.

The people of the Andes had their own unbelievable stories to tell. They told Alexander and Aimé about the mysterious Lake Guatavita, which was believed to harbor colossal riches in its depths. It was said that ancient people, holding the lake to be sacred, had tossed gold into the water to appease their gods. However, no such treasure had ever been discovered, even though the Spanish had once built a canal to drain the lake in search of it. Always skeptical about such rumors, Alexander nonetheless had to go see the famous lake for himself. But he also did not find so much as a single piece of gold.

The journey continued. Alexander and Aimé finally said goodbye to their friends in Bogotá who sent along a group of porters, a dozen mules, and plenty of supplies. This support allowed Alexander and Aimé to carry their equipment through the rugged alpine wilderness. Their latest collection of plants and minerals had already grown extensively since their passage along the Magdalena River.

The path through the Andes was a constant series of steep ups and downs. At times, the group had to cross sweltering tropical valleys. Then they were once again trudging up mountains and over passes pummeled by snowstorms. Whenever the path led along cliff edges, Alexander worried about his precious instruments. Fortunately, the mules knew the way and safely carried all their supplies along the trail.

High up in the Andes, they hiked beneath the watchful eye of the mighty condors, the predatory birds of the mountains. Alexander and Aimé wished they could see the birds up close, but such lords of the sky preferred to soar up near the craggy mountain peaks. From their high perches, the condors seemed to be keeping watch over the small band of travelers, ensuring that they would reach their destination: Quito, a quaint city surrounded by massive volcanoes.

On top of South America

Volcanoes! Alexander had been fascinated by volcanoes ever since he was a young student. And he had become even more entranced by the seething, smoking mountains after climbing the Pico del Teide volcano on Tenerife. But what he saw from the very top of South America surpassed his wildest expectations. An alpine valley stretched across the country of Ecuador, rimmed on both sides by snow-covered peaks pressing skyward. There was row upon row of volcanoes.

"As one ascends into the Andes plateau, these plagues cease. A person can once again breathe air that is fresh and clean."

Quito

"This is an alleyway of volcanoes!" Alexander exclaimed. He was happy that they had decided not to rush to meet the French expedition after all. Instead, the group was now free to explore this mountainous wonderland at their leisure. Of course, what this meant for Alexander was: up close and not from a safe distance. He hoped he might be able to learn more about the inside of Earth and how mountains were formed.

Alexander spent the next six months scrambling up one volcano after another. He had so much energy that Aimé and the other members of the group often got tired and had to quit early or entirely skip some of the excursions to rest. So, the unflagging Alexander hired a few indigenous guides in Quito who would accompany him.

Such ventures could be dangerous. While some of the volcanoes seemed to have gone extinct thousands of years ago, others appeared to be in a kind of temporary sleep. But most of them simmered and seethed from the inside. Some regularly blasted plumes of smoke into the sky, while others, under enormous pressure, sent lava and boulders rocketing up to Earth's surface. Pichincha, Antisana, Iliniza, Cotopaxi, Chimborazo—the mere names of the mountains captivated the two European friends. The peaks towered at more

"In lands where nature is so grand and formidable, one must always be prepared for danger."

than 16,000 feet high. But they were often unreachable due to deep snow or perilous glacial crevasses (a crack in the ice wide enough that a human can slip through, and sometimes hundreds of feet deep!).

Whenever Alexander climbed to the edge of one of the craters, he was able to peer over into a pot of Earth's history. Blue flames rippled at the base of the crater. Blistering hot steam hissed from fissures in the rock, and poisonous gases wafted into the air. It was a good thing that Alexander was as cautious as he was adventurous. He survived all of his volcanic explorations without any injuries.

Alexander had become an expert on volcanoes. No other person in history had ever climbed and studied so many fire-spitting mountains. He was possibly also the most experienced mountain climber of his time, though he didn't even own the most basic climbing equipment: a rope, an ice ax, or hiking boots. Nevertheless, he thought he was well-enough equipped to climb the legendary Chimborazo Mountain, a volcano that is 20,548 feet high. In those days, geographers in the Americas and Europe believed it to be the highest mountain in the world.

Little was yet known about the taller peaks in the Andes Mountains or the Himalayas.

In June 1802, Alexander and Aimé set off for the climb with their mountain guides. They began a slow ascent from the tropical heat of the valley up into cooler temperatures. As they emerged from the forest, they could see the snow-capped peak of the mountain directly in front of them. But there was still a long way to go before they would reach the top. The path eventually got so steep that the group had to leave the mules behind.

A few hours later, a thick fog rolled in and it began to snow. The climbers' hands and feet grew numb from the cold. The indigenous guides refused to go any farther and stayed behind. "We won't let that stop us," Alexander declared.

THE TALLEST MOUNTAINS
We know today that more than twenty mountains in South America are taller than Chimborazo. The tallest mountain on the continent is Aconcagua (at 22,837 feet), on the border of Argentina and Chile. The tallest mountain in North America, Denali in Alaska, is only 20,310 feet above sea level. The true mountain giants of the earth, at over 26,000 feet, are located in the Himalaya mountains in Asia. Mount Everest, the tallest mountain in the world, is about twenty times as tall as the Empire State Building!

The two friends, now forced to shoulder their own supplies, brought along only the most important instruments for measuring. Sometimes they had to climb with their hands or crawl on all fours. They also began to feel the lack of oxygen and had to breathe slowly and deeply to get enough air in their lungs. They became dizzy from headaches and altitude sickness.

Undaunted, Alexander's boundless curiosity pushed him onward. He continued to examine and collect soil samples. Every now and then, he would take out his instruments and measure the temperature, humidity, and air pressure. And as he glanced from the valley up to the mountaintop, he was once again reminded that the earth's climate zones and vegetation change not only depending on latitude, from north to south. There can also be drastic changes at the very same spot on the map as the altitude gets higher or lower. For example, in the three days it had taken them to reach their location high up on Chimborazo mountain, the group had gone from tropical heat to freezing alpine temperatures.

Suddenly, the fog pulled away. The volcano's peak was visible right in front of them. "Only 1,500 more feet until we reach the top," Alexander estimated. But now they could also clearly see the fields of snow and ice ahead of them, crisscrossed with deep crevasses. "We won't be able to get through that," Aimé said, exhausted. To his surprise, Alexander agreed. How he would have loved to summit the colossal mountain, but without the right equipment it was impossible and the risk was too great, even for the unshakable explorer.

Nevertheless, from where they stood high up on the mountain, Alexander and Aimé felt like they were standing on top of South America, or even on top of the world. Due to the difficult conditions, they weren't able to take a precise measurement of how high they had climbed. But they knew they had climbed higher than any other human before them: over 18,000 feet, a world record in 1802. Europe did not have such high mountains as these, and the local people of the Andes did not seem to see much sense in climbing such dangerous mountains. Or perhaps someone local had managed to climb that high too, but it was never recorded or the memory somehow lost. Later climbers would also be challenged by Chimborazo's glaciers, but there would be no records of anyone reaching the peak until eighty years after Alexander's attempted climb.

"A dash of natural cheerfulness, mutual benevolence, and a vivacious sensibility to the majesty of nature do wonders in easing the discomforts of travel."

Onward to the Pacific!

After so many months and adventures in the mountains, it was time to think about moving on. It had now been three years since Alexander and Aimé left Europe. They didn't know if their letters had ever reached home. At least, they had never received any responses. Alexander's instruments had taken a beating from the extreme conditions of their travels, and both men had started to yearn for something a bit more comfortable. They hoped they would find it in Mexico. But in order to get there, they would first have to reach a port harbor along the Pacific coast.

Making their way west, they crossed the equator, which separates the northern hemisphere from the southern. Here they discovered something surprising: When they were north of the equator, the magnetic needle on Alexander's compass pointed north. When they crossed the equator, the needle should have swiveled to point south, toward the magnetic south pole. However, it only pointed south after Alexander and Aimé had walked more than half a mile beyond the equator. "That means," Alexander said excitedly, "that the geographical equator has no influence on the direction of the magnetic needle." He was the first person to discover that there is in fact *another* equator—a magnetic equator—located farther south than the geographical one.

On their journey to the Pacific coast, the two friends often followed paths made by the Incas several hundred years earlier. The Inca were masters at building roads and transport routes through the mountains. Most of the roads were paved with precisely cut ashlars, or stones, some of them more than fifteen feet wide. The roads connected the most remote villages and cities of the Incan Empire. Milestones indicated the distances to the next city.

The roads led Alexander and Aimé to the city of Cajamarca, one of the capital cities of the Incas. Of course, there was not much left of it. Only a few houses and scattered inns had walls that were left standing. Some of them even had baths with hot-water supply lines. Unfortunately, the Spanish conquistadors

Inclinometer for measuring the slope of magnetic lines

"Everything here speaks to the Inca's excellent sensibilities."

had destroyed most of the houses and the royal palace when they plundered the area. Catholic churches now stood on their foundations, and the descendants of the Incas there were forced to live under oppression and work for the Spanish.

Alexander was very curious about the culture and language of these indigenous people. He spoke with some of the descendants from the last Incan emperor, Atahualpa, who had been murdered by the Spanish. His people now lived in poverty. But Alexander could see that several hundred years earlier the Incas had developed a very advanced knowledge of science. They had been able to calculate the course of the stars and were familiar with changes in the climate. A well-organized system of agriculture allowed them to save up supplies for their people in bad times. The more Alexander studied the Incas, the more he appreciated the achievements of their culture. He sketched the ruins of several buildings and took notes of words from their language.

THE INCAS

No other group of peoples on the American continents had amassed as much power as the Incas. Their empire stretched through the Andes from what is now Ecuador to Chile. But then disaster struck: the king's two sons, Atahualpa and Huáscar, began to fight each other for power. At the very same moment, the first Spanish invaders arrived, led by Francisco Pizarro. They exploited the conflict between the two brothers and defeated the Incas in 1532 at the Battle of Cajamarca. They then went on to besiege and plunder the entire empire.

After so many months in the mountains, the two companions longed for a glimpse of the ocean. They could hardly wait to see the Pacific for the first time in their lives from the peaks of the Andes. Every time they crossed a mountain, they thought they might have a chance to catch a glimpse. But their hopes were constantly dashed by a layer of fog that blocked the view. Finally, their eyes were given the sight they had hoped for: The vast Pacific Ocean became visible, stretching out to the horizon. Alexander was ecstatic. He had wanted to see this ocean ever since he was a boy. He had often listened to his friend Georg Forster's stories and had dreamed of his own journey to the Pacific. Now another one of his dreams had come true.

Alexander and Aimé arrived at the Peruvian coastal city of Lima. But the city proved to be a disappointment. "This is the ugliest place we have come across in America," Alexander complained. The ocean and coastline were often closed in by a lingering layer of fog. The Spanish nobles led plush lives and behaved like they were superior, looking down their noses in an intolerable way at everyone else. As soon as they could, the two travelers hopped on a ship that took them north to the port city of Guayaquil.

As they sailed, Alexander stumbled across what would be one of his most famous discoveries. As usual, he stayed above deck most of the trip, fiddling with his instruments. He was constantly measuring the temperatures and sea currents. In doing so, he soon noticed that the water here was much colder than it should have been in tropical regions. By nearly fifty degrees.

The expert scientist immediately came up with an explanation: He believed that a cold current must be flowing north from the icy Antarctic, along the

South American coast all the way up to the equator. He was right. To this day, this current carries tremendous populations of fish and algae from the south polar seas. Where the cold stream meets the warmer waters of the tropics, the marine animals have more food than any other place in the world. The sheer amount of fish is staggering, something that the Peruvian fishing peoples had already known for centuries. But Alexander was the first person who could explain why. This cold current was later named the Humboldt Current after the explorer (though today some refer to it as the Peru Current instead). Humboldt himself didn't like that they named it after him. He wasn't one to chase titles from his many findings in foreign lands.

Alexander and Aimé arrived in Guayaquil to sensational news. The volcano Cotopaxi had recently started erupting, spilling out lava, smoke, and ash. It was less than two hundred miles away. Only a few months earlier, the two friends had been scrambling about on this same mountain. But back then it had been asleep.

Alexander could hardly contain his excitement. A chance to observe a volcanic eruption up close—he simply couldn't pass up such an opportunity. But Aimé was more realistic: "No more change of plans! We need to get on a ship to Mexico, and the next one leaves in a few days. If we miss it, it will be months before the next one leaves because of the rainy season and storms." With a heavy heart, Alexander gave up this once-in-a-lifetime opportunity. Still, from their location at the coast, the two friends could hear the bursts and explosions of the volcano and watch the columns of smoke pushing upward into the sky.

Chapter 5

THE VOYAGE HOME
The land of silver

Only two years later than planned, Alexander von Humboldt and Aimé Bonpland arrived in Mexico. They considered their adventures and experiences along the Orinoco River and in the Andes Mountains well worth the long delay. Mexico was still called New Spain in those days. It was Spain's most important and valuable colony in the Americas. Florida, Texas, and California were also still under Spanish colonial rule. The capital of Mexico, Mexico City, had blossomed into an enormous metropolis, the biggest city in all of the Americas.

The ship from Guayaquil dropped Alexander and Aimé off in Acapulco. The harbor was overfilled with boats, since the city was the starting point for trade between the Americas and the Spanish colony in the Philippines. Alexander and Aimé gathered their things and quickly headed over the mountains toward Mexico's capital city. Alexander was looking forward to having two more volcanoes at his doorstep: Popocatépetl and Iztaccíhuatl. Both looked majestic with their snow-covered peaks.

MEXICO CITY

The capital of Mexico. With twenty million inhabitants in its metropolitan area, today it is one of the largest cities in the world—and the largest in North America. Originally known as Tenochtitlán, the city was created by the Aztecs in 1325 and was the capital of the Aztec Empire until the Spanish invaded in 1521. In 1821, just six years after Humboldt's visit, Mexico would launch the beginning of the Mexican War of Independence, demanding the end of 300 years of Spanish misrule.

Popocatépetl was arguably the most beautiful and striking of the two thousand active and extinct volcanoes in Mexico. The local people believed the volcano acted as a guardian and protector of

"One gets used to sleeping peacefully on a cliff edge."

the city. Of course, Alexander also saw the danger of such a close mountain neighbor: If the volcano were to erupt, the city inhabitants would be threatened by lava and ash flows. But no one wanted to listen to his warnings. The city people chose to live with the risk, and the population kept growing. The volcano was peaceful for the time being.

After their exciting adventures, the two traveling companions were able to relax for a while. Alexander and Aimé finally had time to compile their notes and organize their collection of minerals, rocks, and plants. Mexico City felt almost as much like home as Europe. The streets were clean with sidewalks on both sides and were lit up at night by lanterns. They found their lodging to be very comfortable and the food delicious. Whenever they walked through the marketplace, both men were amazed at the huge mounds of produce: bananas, peaches, pineapples, tomatoes, and corn. Every market stand was decorated with fresh flowers. It was a colorful, cheerful, vivacious city.

The Baron von Humboldt had also made the headlines here. The newspapers had written in detail about his ambitious expedition, as never before had a researcher undertaken such a long and perilous journey across the country. Never before had a scientist ventured into such remote regions, and never before had the geography, climate, flora, and fauna of the Americas been studied with such interest and precision. It was therefore not surprising that the two explorers found themselves welcomed into the homes of the most distinguished Spanish families. The city libraries opened their doors to the men, who took the opportunity to discuss their findings with other scientists around the clock.

Whereas their travels on the Orinoco and in the Andes required the explorers to grapple with nature, their stay in Mexico now had them examining the life, work, and economy of the people. It didn't take Alexander long to realize that New Spain was one of the richest countries in the world. Nowhere else on the globe had as much gold and silver, copper, iron, and quicksilver as Mexico. The country had more than three hundred areas with mines. This naturally piqued the interest of the former mining inspector. Once again, as he had done during his studies, Alexander climbed down through several of the mines, offering suggestions and improvements to the local mine owners. Even in those days, the vast majority of silver in the world was extracted from Mexican mines. "You could mine much more if you used modern methods," the European expert advised them.

ECOLOGICAL INSIGHTS

For many centuries to present day humans have exploited nature with little thought to the consequences. Humboldt was one of the first to recognize the significant interconnectedness of all living organisms. He warned that intrusions in one place could have dramatic consequences in many other places, such as drought, flooding, or hurricanes. Two hundred years later, the effects of global climate change make his insights more relevant than ever.

The landscape above the mines was rich as well. "If you so desired, you could supply the entire world from your soil," Alexander often remarked to his hosts, "with sugar, coffee, cacao, and wine, with wheat, cotton, silk, and hemp." But he also saw the enormous damage that had been done to the landscape. The conquistadores had cut down great swaths of forests without replanting any trees or vegetation. This is the reason why some parts of Mexico today are plagued with extreme drought and barren soil.

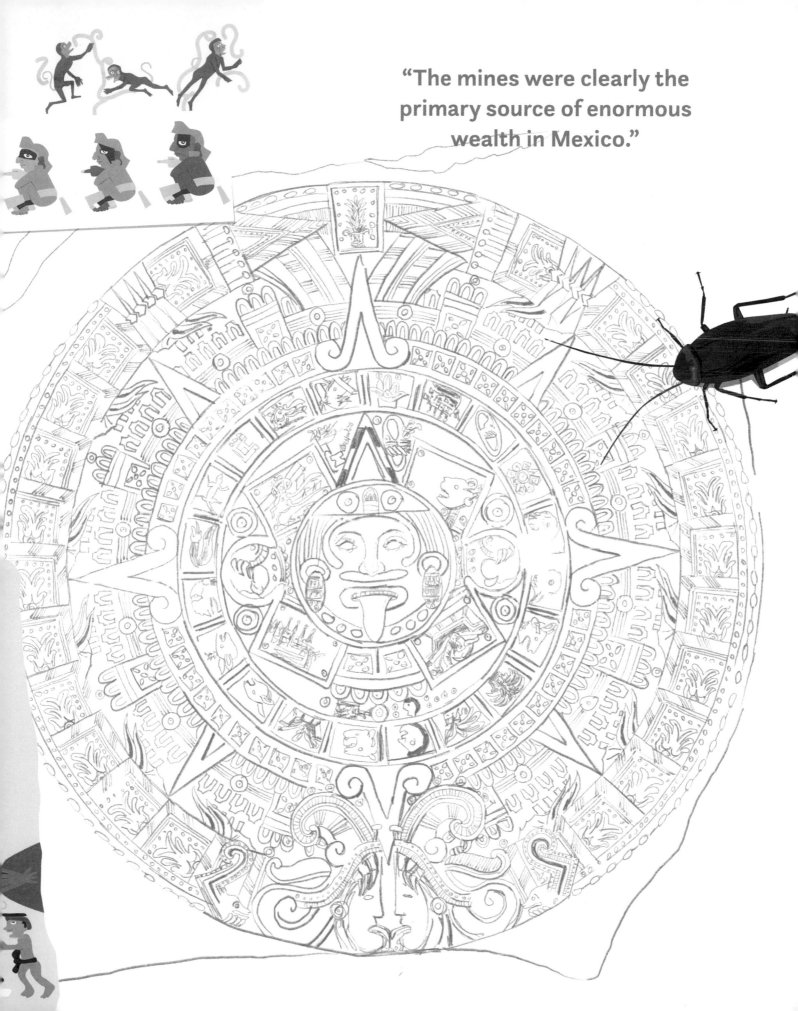

"The mines were clearly the primary source of enormous wealth in Mexico."

Alexander was fascinated by the *chinampas*, floating gardens, and fields in Lake Texcoco at the edge of Mexico City. The Aztecs had developed this sustainable agricultural system long before the Spanish arrived. "It's a wonderful idea," Alexander acknowledged, "that instead of watering the fields, you simply build the fields in the water." Small islands constructed from piled reeds, branches, and silt, eventually anchored by the roots into the lake bed, were planted with flowers, fruits, and vegetables. Some of the chinampas were solid enough to hold a hut. The capital city was well supplied with food from the chinampas, which allowed for multiple harvests per year.

Alexander and Aimé visited another remnant of the indigenous cultures at the Teotihuacán pyramids outside the city. A hundred thousand inhabitants used to live in a city around the pyramids. Now only a few structures remained, but these were gigantic. The Pyramid of the Sun is 213 feet high, only slightly taller than the nearby Pyramid of the Moon. "How long must it have taken to build these colossal structures?" Aimé was amazed at the achievements of the lapsed civilization.

Both Alexander and Aimé climbed the steps to the top of the Pyramid of the Sun, where they could take in a dazzling view. It wasn't hard to imagine how colorful and lively the city must have been long ago. "More proof that the indigenous peoples were not primitive. Theirs was a magnificent culture," Alexander wrote in his notebook. What a pity, then, that the Teotihuacán civilization had vanished completely with only a few ruins left behind. The descendants were now living in dire poverty. Just as in the rest of South America, the local people had also been oppressed and exploited by the Spanish invaders. Such a bitter

CONQUISTADOR...

...is the Spanish word for "conqueror." This was the title the leaders and their soldiers bestowed on themselves in the sixteenth and seventeenth centuries as they invaded Cuba, Mexico, and South America, battling the indigenous peoples and making their lands into Spanish colonies. While the Spanish praised themselves for their courage, the defeated indigenous peoples suffered from their cruelty.

reality made Alexander sad. He continued to advocate for better treatment of the indigenous peoples. But the wealthy landowners wouldn't hear it. They were able to earn a lot of money by forcing the local people to work hard for little pay.

"To observe the Mexican indigenous peoples as a group, one sees nothing but a portrait of great misery."

Although Alexander was concerned about the past and present, he was also always looking forward to the future. He had a vision after studying a map of New Spain: The land of Mexico was bound on both sides by large oceans. *What if a canal were to be built linking both of the oceans?* he asked himself. This would allow ships to pass from one ocean to the other without having to sail all the way around the tip of South America, an enormous detour. Passengers could reach their destinations more quickly, and trade would certainly benefit from the faster route.

Because Alexander was more than just a dreamer, he immediately began drawing up concrete plans. He detailed nine possible canal routes on the map. The drawings had to be done on-site, the landscape measured, and the best path chosen. When he told his Spanish hosts about his idea, they thought he was crazy. However, one hundred years later, Alexander's idea became reality. One of the routes that he suggested long ago is now a waterway: the famous Panama Canal, one of the most important shipping lanes in the world.

Basaltic prisms line the ravine beneath the Santa María Regla waterfall in Mexico.

An American president

Alexander and Aimé remained in Mexico for more than a year. They had now been traveling for five years in total. They started to think about returning home to Europe. But first they wanted to visit Cuba, where they had left some of their collections and notes three years earlier. They would first have to go back to get them.

Having arrived in Cuba with plans to look for a ship to take them to Europe, Alexander immediately had another change of heart. Before going home, he decided he simply had to visit the United States in North America, where a certain Thomas Jefferson was president. Jefferson was not only a politician but also a respected academic, architect, and inventor who had traveled far and wide and had even once worked as an ambassador in Paris. Now would be the perfect opportunity to meet him. Alexander was certain Jefferson would be interested in their experiences.

"You must be joking," Aimé moaned. "Not another change of plans!" But, as always, he went along. They needed forty large crates to pack all the objects and samples they had gathered during their travels. The two friends set out with their enormous pile of baggage to Philadelphia, which was then the second-largest city in the US.

During their sea voyage from Cuba, their ship passed through one of the worst storms they had ever experienced. A hurricane chased the ship across the ocean for days, causing the masts and sails to shudder from the force. "If only we had sailed directly home. If only we hadn't come on this useless detour!" wailed the frightened Aimé. He was afraid for his life. But the storm didn't seem to rattle Alexander. He loved to travel, he was in his element, and he considered danger a part of the experience. Mostly he worried about his collections and manuscripts. "We have carried the collection everywhere we've gone and managed to preserve it; it has to make it back to Paris in one piece," he wrote hopefully. Fortune was on their side. After great difficulties, Alexander and Aimé's ship was finally able to reach the Philadelphia harbor.

"Perhaps I shall die on the edge
of a crater or be swallowed up
by an ocean wave."

THE UNITED STATES OF AMERICA

In 1776, the thirteen North American British colonies declared independence from England and founded the United States of America. At the time of Humboldt's visit, the US was only a small country at the edge of the East Coast. It wasn't until much later that the country stretched all the way to the Pacific Ocean. Today the US comprises fifty states, two commonwealths, and multiple territories and is one of the most powerful nations in the world.

The news about Baron von Humboldt and his expedition across South America and Mexico reached North America ahead of the travelers. Everyone was eager to meet them. To hear their stories. To learn from their experiences. President Jefferson was no exception. He issued an invitation for the renowned explorers to come visit him in Washington, DC. The newly established capital city with only five thousand inhabitants was little more than a village at that time.

The city had been established on the border between the northern and southern states as a compromise between competing political parties. At first, people were reluctant to move to the capital because the summers were stiflingly hot, and the swampy land attracted swarms of mosquitoes. The streets were muddy and full of puddles. There was scaffolding everywhere for the many construction projects. *Was this really to be the capital of such a large nation?* Aimé asked himself. He was much more used to Paris. However, this was only the very start of the young country.

Even the White House, where the president lived, was still under construction. A few rooms could already be used, and this is where Thomas Jefferson welcomed the Baron von Humboldt. In their conversations, Alexander praised the freedom and democracy of North America. He hoped Europe would one day adopt a democratic system and get rid of monarchies and emperors that did not give the people much say. Alexander also criticized the brutal treatment of slaves in the Spanish colonies. President Jefferson's brow furrowed when Alexander talked about this. Jefferson did not like that topic, since he himself owned several slaves who were forced to work on his plantation.

Jefferson quickly changed the subject to Alexander's research and discoveries from the past five years. As president, he had a special interest in such information because the Spanish colonialists were the direct neighbors of the US. However, despite their proximity, Jefferson knew very little about what was taking place in South America. Alexander gladly shared his maps and his findings with Jefferson. His own topographical maps were more precise than those of the Spanish government. He told Jefferson about the fertile lands of Mexico and the country's wealthy mines. But Jefferson was also interested in hearing about their adventures—from the river exploration of the Orinoco, to the expedition up the Chimborazo volcano, to the hurricane along the Cuban coast. The US president admitted that he had learned more about South America from this Prussian baron than he had gleaned from all his studies and books on the topic.

SLAVERY

By the start of the nineteeth century, the slave trade was a well-established practice in the Americas and in several other places across the globe. The indigenous peoples and black Africans were considered inferior races and inhumanely bought and sold. Most white people at the time regarded such treatment as perfectly natural. One of the few white people who was disgusted by slavery was Alexander von Humboldt. Again and again he criticized the fate of the slaves and advocated for their freedom and equality. In his most famous work, Cosmos, he wrote, "In maintaining the unity of the human race we also reject the disagreeable assumption of superior and inferior peoples.... All are equally entitled to freedom."

A global citizen in Europe

A ship called *Favorite* brought Alexander and Aimé back to Europe in the summer of 1804. Even their forty shipping crates full of notes and plants and minerals survived the long sea voyage. They landed in the French port city of Bordeaux and continued on toward Paris. Both men felt melancholy now that their great adventure had come to an end. However, the celebratory reception of the explorers in France helped them forget their sadness. Now was the time to look ahead to the future.

"When are you returning to Berlin?" Aimé asked his friend. "Berlin?" replied Alexander, "I think I'll stay in Paris for now." This made Aimé very happy. It would take both of them together to study their enormous collection of plants. And Paris also had the very best printers and publishers, which they hoped would publish their books. In addition, Paris was home to the largest population of scientists in the world in those days. Alexander was eager to discuss his discoveries with them. But his brother, Wilhelm, his friends in Berlin, and even the Prussian king were not very happy to hear about his decision. "As a German citizen, he should come back and live in his own country," they protested. But Alexander refused, claiming: "I'm a global citizen now!"

For the next twenty years, Alexander lived mostly in Paris. He held lectures at the universities. Discussed the future of the Americas with young people. Wrote dozens of books that were translated into dozens of languages. Everyone praised his sketches of the volcanoes, Incan ruins, and indigenous scripts. But he did not make much of a living from his books and lectures. His costs became so high that he had to spend most of his remaining fortune. Copyright laws were not yet in place in those days, and so Alexander hardly earned anything from the many pirated copies and

"My expedition of over 9,000 miles was an unparalleled joy."

translations of his books. But wherever he went, he was praised and admired. The people were enraptured by his stories of the Orinoco and Chimborazo. No one else had ever talked about such adventures with so much detail. Readers all over Europe were ecstatic. President Jefferson sent his praise from the US. Baron Alexander von Humboldt had become an international star.

In South America, the people began to refer to him as the "second discoverer of America." No one else on Earth was as familiar with the South American continent. From Mexico to Argentina, from Cuba to Chile, Alexander became a revered figure. Streets and schools were named after him. Several cities erected statues in his honor.

Even in the midst of all the honors and recognition, the gray-haired scholar continued to dream of visiting far-off places. Sometimes he even wished he had stayed in the Americas.

Alexander began to plan his next travels. He wanted to go to Italy, Greece, Spain, and Mexico. But his main priority was a much larger, much more distant destination: the Himalayas in Asia. If he went there, he could find out whether or not the peaks of the Andes really were the highest mountains in the world. No scientist had ever measured or climbed these mountains.

"THE SECOND DISCOVERER"

In Humboldt's day, Columbus was widely regarded as the "first discoverer" of the Americas. In fact, however, we know that he wasn't. Indigenous peoples had long been around. Columbus's "discovery" simply made the continent known to Europeans for the first time. Nevertheless, throughout history many landmarks, statues, buildings, and more would be named after white Europeans like Columbus and Humboldt to honor their "discoveries." But 90 percent of the indigenous population died as a result of the Americas being "discovered" by Europe, and those who survived were treated horribly by colonizers. Because of this fact, many people choose to no longer honor the "discovery of America," for example celebrating "Indigenous Peoples' Day" rather than "Columbus Day."

THE HIMALAYAS

What Humboldt did not yet know, but perhaps had already suspected, was that the Himalayas contained the highest and mightiest mountains in the world. Ten peaks are over 26,000 feet, including Mount Everest. At 29,029 feet, it is the highest mountain in the world. But Chimborazo in South America holds a different world record: Because the mountain is located at the equator, where the globe bulges slightly outward, its peak is the farthermost point from the center of Earth.

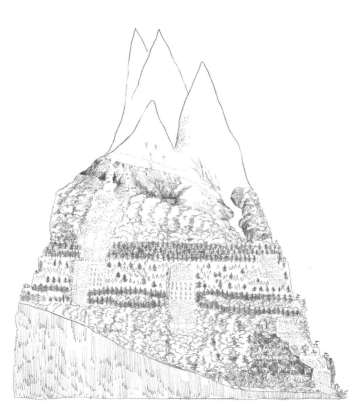

The only passage to the Himalayas led across India, which was under British colonial rule in those days. Alexander went to London to ask permission for his journey. Once again, he was celebrated, asked to give lectures, and invited to parties. But all of his social connections were in vain, and he was denied permission to travel through India. The British rulers were afraid Alexander might act as a spy for his country. But the baron refused to give up. He traveled a second time to London to try convincing the authorities. All to no avail.

Prussian soldier

Meanwhile, the Prussian king was putting pressure on Alexander to finally return to Berlin, threatening to withhold his annual pension if he did not. Alexander needed the money because he had long since spent his inheritance and any earnings from his books. After five years in the Americas and twenty years in Paris, he decided to return home. He was almost fifty years old. In Berlin, like everywhere he went, he found himself in high demand. Everyone clamored to hear his stories. He was regularly asked to attend the court of the king, who liked to decorate himself with his most famous subjects. Alexander did not particularly enjoy all the fuss made over him. However, his return to Berlin proved to be a stroke of good luck. He was offered another opportunity to travel to a far-off, little-explored land.

The second man

The world applauded Alexander von Humboldt: his research travels, his books, his great service to science, his knowledge about the cultures of the Americas. He inspired the explorers and artists of his day. He had climbed Chimborazo. He had proved the link between the Orinoco and Amazon Rivers. He had discovered the Humboldt (or Peru) Current. He had met with a US president.

But what happened to the second man who had traveled with Alexander: Aimé Bonpland? We should not forget about him. After all, Aimé had gone along with Alexander from the very beginning. He had even been with Alexander when they started planning their adventures. And he was with him paddling through the jungle in a canoe, climbing up mountains, and surviving terrible storms.

Aimé had collected most of the 60,000 plant varieties that the two men had brought back to Europe. He was the one who had sorted and described them in an orderly fashion. He had even agreed to go along with most of Alexander's changes of plans, though sometimes less than enthusiastically. And he had never given up, even when he fell very ill along the way. Following their return, Aimé had also been heaped with medals and honors. Still, he would always remain in the shadow of the famous Baron von Humboldt.

A microscope for botanical studies

Back in France, Aimé took a position as superintendent of the imperial gardens at Malmaison, just west of Paris. But he was not cut out to be a custodian; he was a restless explorer. Just like Alexander, Aimé pined for further adventures. And so, he decided to go abroad again, this time to Argentina in the southern part of South America. And this time without his famous friend. Instead, he brought along his entire library and hundreds of plants and seeds in his bags.

Fate was not always kind to Aimé. He moved to the jungle on the Río Paraná, a river that reminded him of the Orinoco. It was here that he came across an important discovery: The indigenous peoples gathered a wild plant which they used to brew a powerful tea as medicine to treat various illnesses. They called the shrub yerba maté. Of course, the plant stirred Aimé's interest as a doctor

"Throughout his agonizing illness, Monsieur Bonpland displayed great courage and kindness of character, traits which he never abandoned, even in the most mortifying of situations."

and botanist. He thought it might be a good business venture to export the tea leaves to Europe. With such an idea in mind, he founded a colony for growing and harvesting the yerba maté shrubs.

These plans, however, proved disastrous for Aimé. In the neighboring country of Paraguay, the reigning dictator who had a monopoly on maté was unhappy with Aimé's plans. The dictator wanted to maintain control over the cultivation and trade of the tea himself. He sent his soldiers to Aimé's colony, where they evicted the indigenous peoples and took the Frenchman captive. Aimé was a prisoner for almost ten years in the jungle and had no outside contact with friends or family during that time. Even the international protests by influential politicians and scientists could do little to free him. The famous Alexander von Humboldt could not help him either.

When he was finally released, Aimé Bonpland was given multiple offers to return to Europe for work. But he wanted to stay in South America. He pursued one project after the next: breeding sheep in Uruguay; cultivating orange trees in the south of Brazil. He finally returned to the Río Paraná, where he died at the age of eighty-five in May 1858, one year before the death of his good friend Alexander von Humboldt, in Berlin. Against all odds, he had managed to live a long and full life.

YERBA MATÉ

The tea made from the dried leaves of the maté shrub is the beloved national drink of Argentina, Uruguay, and Paraguay. It is even a drink many people enjoy in the US today, though it remains relatively unknown in many places in the world. Its stimulating effects are similar to coffee, and it can be similarly drunk either hot or cold, though its taste is very different.

The village where Aimé spent the end of his life is now named after him: Bonpland. Other things bear his name as well: a mountain in Venezuela; a street in Buenos Aires; a type of squid; a variety of orchid; and even a crater on the moon. But this list is short compared to everything that has been named after Humboldt. To this day, Aimé remains the second man, always in the shadow of the world-famous baron.

Perhaps Aimé was never as famous and successful as his friend Alexander. But, unlike his friend, he got to spend the final forty years of his life in the place that his friend Alexander had always hoped to revisit: in the tropics and jungles of South America.

Chapter 6

New Adventures
A whirlwind trek through Siberia

Theodolite, an instrument for measuring angles

The Russian emperor Tsar Nicholas I had also heard about the world-renowned Alexander von Humboldt's journeys. The tsar knew that Alexander had been a mining inspector in his early days and was thus familiar with diamonds, gold, and other precious metals. He hoped to be able to exploit Alexander's knowledge in order to increase the wealth of his own vast country. The Russian finance minister informed the tsar that the German scholar was pining for another great adventure. Alexander soon received an invitation from the tsar to travel and explore the great realm of Russia. The trip would be all expenses paid.

Alexander immediately made plans to travel from Berlin to Saint Petersburg and Moscow and then deep into the wilds of Siberia, which brush up close to the Himalaya Mountains. *Maybe,* Humboldt thought, *I could change my plans during the trip and take a tiny little detour.* He didn't waste any time in accepting the offer, and very soon he was off. Although nearly sixty years old, Alexander was in as good health and shape as he had ever been.

Crossing the seemingly endless Siberian steppe is a bold and dangerous mission. From the start, the journey took a different turn than Alexander had planned. The tsar had organized the expedition based on his own interests. He provided a group of mountain climbers to the Baron von Humboldt. But Alexander quickly realized the guides were not there only to help him. In fact, they were mainly present to monitor his progress and to make him stay on the fixed route.

Alexander was thus not free to decide where to stop or what to see. As always, he was fascinated by the plants and rocks that lined the way. He wanted to add to his collection, to take out his instruments, and to measure things. But his guides pressed him onward, always to the next mining site. There, they urged him to analyze which metals might be found there and how the mine could be improved. "Could we perhaps speak with the miners or the farmers?" he asked his guides. "No way!" came the response. "Such people live wretched lives and who wants to hear about that?"

The band of travelers thus pressed ahead as if in a mad dash through the enormous country. Day and night, almost without pause. There were no cities here, and they drove straight past any small settlements without stopping. However, they frequently paused to change horses at the numerous post offices

SIBERIA

Just beyond the Ural Mountains begins the enormous Siberian landscape. It stretches to the North all the way to the Arctic Ocean, to the east to the Pacific, and to the south to Mongolia and China. Gigantic rivers such as the Ob and the Lena flow through the endless steppes (flat grasslands). Although some large cities now exist in Siberia, such as Omsk and Novosibirsk, most of the area is covered by an overwhelming sense of loneliness. To travel here is still an adventure.

spread out at great intervals in the land. On and on they went, until finally reaching the city of Tobolsk along the great Irtysh River. This was to be the final destination on their itinerary and from here they would turn around and go back. But Alexander had other ideas. He wanted the chance to explore at least one Asian mountain range. The closest were the Altai Mountains. Overriding the tsar's instructions, he plotted a course east with his group of mountain guides.

Tsar Nicholas I,
Russian emperor

At some point, the Altai Mountains began to rise up on the horizon. They had almost made it to China, over three thousand miles from Berlin.

At the sight of the peaks, Alexander could no longer be held back by the guides. He marched tirelessly toward the mountains. He crawled into caves. Scooped up rocks and minerals. Dried and sorted plants. Such activities stirred memories of his time spent in South America. At 15,000 feet high, the peaks here were not nearly as high as Chimborazo. Still, Alexander was able to find rare animals, plants, and rocks.

Eventually his travel companions pressed him to stop. The summer was coming to an end and the Siberian winter was no time for exploring. The heaps of snow alone made passage impossible. In addition, the tsar was anxious to receive Alexander's reports. They allowed him one final detour on his return journey: to the Caspian Sea. One of the largest inland lakes in the world, it was yet another of Alexander's childhood dreams. Not only was he now given the chance to view the sea from the shoreline, he was also able to explore it by ship as well.

"**I feel stronger, more active than ever.**"

After that, the travelers raced in their wagons back toward Saint Petersburg, to the court of the tsar. The expedition had covered over 12,000 miles in eight months—most likely a world record at that time. But such merits were not important to Alexander. He would rather have traveled more slowly and taken more time along the way. Stopped more often to examine the many marvels. Still, he was happy that he had been given another opportunity to travel the world once more. His whirlwind Siberian trip was to be the second but also the last great expedition of his life. Along the way he had learned many new things, and he was able to add to his botanical and geological collections. And in addition, he had brought back a lot of useful information for the tsar.

Carl Friedrich Gauss
(1777–1855):

The "Prince of mathematicians" was not only known for geometry and computational equations, but also as an astronomer who contributed to important celestial discoveries. He was a professor at the University of Gottingen and director of the observatory there.

Simón Bolívar
(1783–1830):

As "El Libertador," the liberator, he led the fight for independence of the South American colonies against Spain. His dream of a united Latin America was never realized.

Caroline von Humboldt
(1766–1829):

The wife of Alexander's brother, Wilhelm, was considered an independent woman by the standards of those days. She traveled alone throughout Europe and held literary salons at their residences in Berlin, Paris, and Rome, inviting and keeping up a correspondence with the greatest minds of the era.

Charles Darwin
(1809–1882):

Like Humboldt, the British naturalist circled the globe for many years, primarily via ship. During his travels, his findings laid the foundation for his groundbreaking theory of evolution, which stated that nature has evolved over millions of years by the continual adaptation of living beings to their environment.

Joseph Gay-Lussac
(1778–1850):

The French chemist and physicist was primarily concerned with the interaction of temperature, heat, and gases and through his studies was able to express some important laws of nature. Together with Humboldt, he experimented with electricity and water.

Johann Wolfgang von Goethe
(1749–1832):

Known as the greatest German poet, he generated an enormous number of poems, novels, and plays, but his work also touched on the natural sciences. Sometimes his scientific theories contradicted Humboldt's findings and they eventually turned out to be false.

Friedrich Schelling
(1775–1854):

One of the most important German philosophers of his time. In addition to questions about thinking, he also applied himself to scientific problems. He thus attracted the interest of the young Humboldt, who felt a deep connection to him throughout his entire life.

The world comes to Berlin

Back in Berlin after his Russia adventure, Alexander von Humboldt decided it was time to gather all of his knowledge and experiences into one large book. He titled it *Cosmos* because he wanted it to be a comprehensive description of the whole of nature. He had traveled through Europe, the Americas, and Asia. Survived journeys by ship across big oceans. Crossed steppes, explored jungles, and climbed mountains and volcanoes. He had debated with famous scientists and political leaders. Collected and examined more plants and rocks than he could count. Alexander von Humboldt knew the world perhaps better than anyone else.

But bringing such an enormous amount of knowledge into a practical order was no easy task. Whenever he started working on a particular topic, he quickly realized he was lacking some necessary information. He asked other scholars for their help. He met with colleagues from around the globe in Berlin. He wrote letters to Saint Petersburg, Cuba, Mexico, Venezuela, Philadelphia, and Washington, DC—wherever he needed more information. For several years he wrote thousands of letters. And he received many more in return. He even got letters from his old friend Aimé Bonpland in Argentina. Aimé sent him information about plants he had found deep in the southern part of the continent. Alexander no longer had to travel around the world. The world now came to him in Berlin.

WORLD WIDE WEB
Not only did Humboldt travel around the world, he also built up a worldwide network of scholars and scientists who exchanged information with him, answered his questions, and participated in discussions. They included Thomas Jefferson and Simón Bolívar, the poet Friedrich Schiller, the mathematician Carl Friedrich Gauss, the chemist Gay-Lussac, and the philosopher Friedrich Schelling. Goethe even considered Humboldt the most significant conversational partner of his life.

His book project continued to progress, though there seemed to be no good place to end it. He was constantly receiving new tips and data that he wanted to include. After ten years of writing, Alexander finally decided to publish a first volume of his book: *Cosmos*. It was a resounding success, an international bestseller. It was translated into English, French, Spanish, Italian, Russian, Danish, Polish, *and* Hungarian.

The reason that *Cosmos* was so well loved is that it was not just a boring old book about science. It was rather a thrilling story that took the reader on an adventure around the whole surface of Earth. Up the most gigantic landscapes like mountains and volcanoes, but also down to the smallest reaches where insects and diamonds can be found. It also described the history of people and their migration across the globe. And to top it all off, the book gazed upward into the universe, describing the solar system and the distant stars. Alexander von Humboldt transported the reader. People living in the remotest villages were now connected to the rest of the world. And he told his stories and explanations in such an exciting way that readers immediately wished to set off on their own adventures.

The book shows the ways in which everything in the universe is connected. That humans make up only a tiny piece of the puzzle. That even a hidden seed or very small insect can have an important role to play in the "network of life," as Humboldt called it. All things great and small, the earth and sky, mountains and dust, oceans and singular water drops, ancient trees and beetles—everything is interconnected and depends on everything else. Taken all together, these things make up our world, our cosmos.

Alexander had hardly put down his pen after writing the first volume of *Cosmos* when he picked it up again and began writing the second. In total, he wrote five volumes in over twenty years up until the time of his death on May 6, 1859, in Berlin. He was almost ninety years old. The enormous crowd that came for his funeral in Berlin was the largest gathering the city had seen in years. The people came to pay their last respects to a man they regarded as the greatest explorer and traveler of the century. And they often referred to him with a quotation which, though it is uncertain whether or not he actually ever said it, nevertheless perfectly sums up Alexander von Humboldt's way of thinking:

"The most dangerous worldviews are the worldviews of people who have never viewed the world."

Humboldt.

Books

Humboldt, Alexander von. *Personal Narrative of Travels to the Equinoctial Regions of the New Continent*. Translated by Helen Maria Williams. Cambridge: Cambridge University Press, 2011.

———. *Selected Writings*. Edited by Andrea Wulf. New York: Everyman's Library, 2018.

———. *Views of the Cordilleras and Monuments of the Indigenous Peoples of the Americas*. Edited by Vera M. Kutzinski and Ottmar Ette. Chicago: University of Chicago Press, 2013.

———. *Views of Nature*. Edited by Stephen T. Jackson and Laura Dassow Walls, translated by Mark W. Person. Chicago: University of Chicago Press, 2014.

Kehlmann, Daniel. *Measuring the World: A Novel*. New York: Vintage Books, 2007.

Lack, Walter H. *Alexander von Humboldt: The Botanical Exploration of the America*. New York: Prestel Publishing, 2018.

Wulf, Andrea. *The Adventures of Alexander von Humboldt*. New York: Pantheon Graphic Library, 2019.

———. *The Invention of Nature: Alexander von Humboldt's New World*. New York: Alfred A. Knopf, 2015.

Audio & Video

Casper, Gerhard. *A Young Man from "Ultima Thule" visits Jefferson: Alexander von Humboldt in Philadelphia and Washington.* Filmed November 2009 at the American Philosophical Society in Philadelphia. Video, 1:06:43. diglib.amphilsoc.org/islandora/object/video:1035

Wulf, Andrea. *Humboldt—the Inventor of Nature.* Discovery BBC World Service. Audio, 27:00. bbc.co.uk/programmes/p039mhx5

Museums

Humboldt Museum
Located in the city of Humboldt in Saskatchewan, Canada (named after him in 1875), this museum focuses on featuring and preserving the city's local art and history.
humboldtmuseum.ca

Humboldt's birthplace
Today it is the Berlin-Brandenburg Academy of Sciences and Humanities.
bbaw.de/en/

Humboldt's childhood home and grave site
The Humboldt Museum, located at Tegel Palace.
museumsportal-berlin.de/en/museums/humboldt-museum-schloss-tegel

The Humboldt Forum
A place of knowledge and exchange in the spirit of Humboldt.
On display are exhibitions on non-European cultures.
humboldtforum.com/en

Websites

edition-humboldt.de

A project by the Berlin-Brandenburg Academy of Sciences and Humanities to digitize Humboldt's journals and other documents.

avhumboldt.de

This information platform provides materials, activities, and projects involving Humboldt.

humboldt.staatsbibliothek-berlin.de

The Humboldt Portal of the Berlin State Library provides information on Humboldt's life and work.

VOLKER MEHNERT *has worked for many years as a freelance journalist, travel writer, and author, and he has lived in Latin America, eastern Europe, and the US, where he has often followed in the footsteps of Alexander von Humboldt. His books about Mexico, California, Portugal, and the South Seas range from topics of tourism and culture to history.*

CLAUDIA LIEB *studied communication design in Münster and at the University of Applied Sciences in Hamburg. She lives in Munich, where she works in a studio cooperative as an illustrator and graphic artist.*
claudialieb.de